A Non-Duality Press

SAMPLER

Issue № 2
2007

NON-DUALITY PRESS
United Kingdom

Cover graphics by John Gustard

Non-Duality Press
6 Folkestone Rd, Salisbury SP2 8JP
United Kingdom
www.non-dualitybooks.com

Isbn 10: 0-9553999-3-9
Isbn 13: 978-0-9553999-3-0

Introduction

Since its inception in 2004, Non-Duality Press has set out to make available the clearest contemporary writing on non-duality to a wider audience.

Each author, in his or her unique way, attempts to express the inexpressible. They point to 'our original face', the ground of being, using everyday language without abstruse jargon, but informed by a depth and width of experience of western and eastern paths. Beyond new-age fads and therapies, these are contemporary expressions of the perennial philosophy.

A Non-Duality Press Sampler contains short biographical introductions to the authors and extracts from each of their books. Wherever possible, references are given to further reading, websites and interviews with the authors, especially from the Dutch *Advaita* webzine, *Amigo.*

The final chapter includes a preview of forthcoming titles for 2007.

If you are new to these writings, we hope you feel inspired to explore the radical perspectives contained in these books.

Julian Noyce
Editor, Non-Duality Press

Contents

Leo Hartong is widely regarded as one of the most eloquent communicators of non-duality. His first book, *Awakening to the Dream*, skillfully maps out the territory to be examined and, with humour and intelligence, gently guides the reader to the heart of the non-dual perception.

His second book, *From Self to Self,* is a compilation of questions, answers and quotations that arose in response to *Awakening to the Dream.* Leo brings a perfect balance of head and heart to a subject that is often too cerebral or too emotional.

Awakening to the Dream

148 pages. Isbn: 0-9547792-1-5 £8.20 / $14.76

From Self to Self

262 pages. Isbn: 0-9547792-7-4 £10.80 / $19.95

Interview
Amigo No.6 (www.ods.nl/am1gos) *Mountains and Valleys*
Amigo No.9

Website, forum and bi-weekly newsletter archive
www.awakeningtothedream.com

"In my book I don't claim that it was written to explain something, instead I quoted an old Dutch saying, which translates as 'The mouth has no choice but to speak of that which fills the heart.' Through such a book, just as through the smell of a rose and everything else, the One shares itself with itself. When all's said and done there actually is only one teacher; and this one is always present. No one is ever without this teacher, and it doesn't matter whether this one appears as intuition, as an event, or as a person."

"*Awakening to the Dream* is both an excellent introduction to Nonduality, and an encounter with an awakened one. The writing style is memorable. This is a valuable work which could become a classic in the field."

Jerry Katz author of *One: Essential Writings on Nonduality*

"Awakening to the Dream is an extraordinarily clear and thoughtful presentation of subject matter that is often experienced as both confusing and paradoxical ... I really enjoyed your use of appropriate quotes, clever analogies/metaphors and the clarity and ease with which you were able to express the inexpressible."

Chuck Hillig, http://www.blackdotpubs.com

"This is a wonderfully clear book pointing you to the direct and immediate realization that you are already Home (and always have been). Amongst spiritual books, it's a rare one in ten million that goes all the way. This one does. Leo goes straight to the heart of the matter. I recommend it highly."

Joan Tollifson, http://www.joantollifson.com

"(Awakening to the Dream) is a marvellous exposition of non-dual teachings, straight from the heart. Read the chapter on the subject of free-will to see how brilliantly Leo puts across the message. Highly recommended!"

Dennis Waite author of *The Book of One* and *Back to the Truth*

"What a gift this book is. Finally someone who delves into the issue of Enlightenment, Awakening, Ego and Advaita with lucid, luminous languaging, not semantic games and mental gymnastics. A clear jewel to be read over and over again."

Amazon.com Reviewer

When a schoolteacher writes 'I' on a blackboard and asks the students what they see, most of them will answer that they see the word 'I.' It's rare for someone to say 'I see a blackboard with 'I' written on it.' Just as the relatively huge blackboard is ignored in favour of a single letter, we ignore the Awareness that is the permanent background to all phenomena. We tend to ignore this in the same way that we forget the screen on which a movie is projected. It is the unchanging characteristic in all the movies we watch, but it never gets involved in the movie, as such. The movie may depict an ocean, a long winding road, a murder, or a forest fire; but the screen will not get wet, move from place to place, bleed, or burn. Likewise, Awareness remains pure and unaffected by its content.

Awareness is the consistent characteristic in and behind all experience, yet it is also that which most easily escapes our attention. Attention is not the same as Awareness. Our brain is designed in such a way that giving attention to something automatically implies ignoring something else. We see the stars and ignore the space; we read this text and ignore the page; we see the movie and ignore the screen; yet it is obvious that the ignored space, page, and screen are as fundamental to our observations as the stars, the text, and the movie, which hold our attention. This is an important point, as the mechanics of attention often get confused with Awareness. Attention works through noticing something in contrast to something that's ignored, while Awareness is the non-dual space that sustains both the noticed and the ignored. Attention may require effort; Awareness simply is. Everything that comes up is contained in and embraced by this Awareness, including objects perceived as 'out there' (rocks, cars, other sentient beings) and emotions, thoughts, and feelings experienced as 'in here.' In this sense, Awareness is as much in the body-mind as the body-mind is in Awareness. Compare it to a clay pot, which contains space and at the same time is contained by space. Breaking the pot will not affect this space.

In the same way, when the body-mind organism dies, nothing happens to Awareness. To see that you are this Awareness is to see that you were never born, never lived, and that you will never die. You *are* the living Awareness, which is the clear and open space in and from which everything arises, including your body-mind and your sense of individuality. No matter where you turn the spotlight of your attention, the floodlight of awareness is already there. It is aware of everything – of your breath going in and out, of the sudden sound, the light, and the falling of a sparrow halfway around the world. Pure Awareness is unconditioned and without attributes; it is simply present with no beginning or end, and it does not require any effort on your part. If you make an effort, Awareness is effortlessly aware of this. All that arises is its content, but this does not affect it any more than a mirror is affected by what it reflects. Like the mirror, Awareness makes no effort to accept or reject anything. It does not judge or take a point of view because it includes all possible points of view. The following poem attributed to the Taoist philosopher Chuang Tzu illustrates this.

> *The wild geese do not intend to cast their reflection:*
> *The water has no mind to receive their image.*

It is only because of the dualistic and linear nature of language that this text appears to split that which is essentially one into Pure Awareness and its content. In reality, there is no such duality.

In this dualistic description, Awareness stands for the permanent, while the appearances in Awareness represent the impermanent; but really they are the two sides of a single coin. However, to speak of two sides is still using two labels for one indefinable something. Perhaps it's a better metaphor to say that the height of the mountain *is* the depth of the valley.

Pure Awareness does not need anything other than itself to be what it is. Contrary to what logic dictates, it does not need an object outside of itself to be aware of. Another way of saying this is that Awareness is both the subject *and* the object. As such Awareness is Self-luminous. It is a Self-sustaining, Self-aware feedback loop, which the use of language seems to split into subject/object, the creator and the created, or Awareness and its content. The Hindus illustrate this with the image of a spider, which produces a web from its own body, plays in it and then draws it back into itself.

The Self is producing, watching, and appearing in and as the grand show of the unfolding cosmic drama, just as a dreamer simultaneously produces, watches, and appears in her dream. You, me, the book, the chair, and the terrorists on the news are all variations in the way Awareness appears to itself, just as the people, the house, the sunrise, and the monsters appearing in a dream are all made of the same dream stuff.

From *Awakening to the Dream*
Chap.11: Who is watching the show?

Question: Everyone says that it's consciousness that seems to appear as everything. I want to ask what is it that makes this consciousness... this oneness... manifest itself in so many forms. What is it that makes the One appear to be many?

I would like to know your reasons for it. Please don't speak from books because I've read many myself. Tell me what you know. That which you have experienced.

Answer: The One appearing AS the many is Self-Originating. It is the Causeless-First-Cause, the Sourceless-Source. It is THAT which brings forth time and space and is itself prior to time and space. It has no why, nor when, nor location, and IT IS, without a reason for being. We could say IT is itself the very reason for all being and non-being.

No label sticks to it and therefore it has been called the void. Even calling it the void is again a label and again just words. Whatever I answer will be words and apparently you have found words to be unable to convey the answer you're looking for.

You ask what my experience is. When you read the book *'Awakening to the Dream'* and the answers in the other newsletters, you'll find that I do not call this 'understanding' an experience for someone, but point to the realization that there is no individual who can have such an experience.

IT is not something that can be put into plain words, so no one can tell you what IT is. It is like asking about the taste of an apple: it cannot be explained. Not because it is something complex, but because words are always symbols for something; they are never the thing itself.

In the case of the apple, words can point you to an apple seller or an apple tree, but the tasting can only be done by you. With your question there can only be a pointing back to the Livingness that allows 'you' to ask this question.

One taste from 'the apple of enlightenment' will dissolve the taster and only taste remains.

One matter, one energy, one Light, one Light-mind,
Endlessly emanating all things.
One turning and burning diamond,
One, one, one.

From: 'The Rumi Collection', *Andrew Harvey*

**From Self to Self*

Chap.14, p.48; What is it that makes the ONE appear to be many?

David Carse: *Perfect Brilliant Stillness* is a remarkable book by a remarkable man. David makes it very clear that he is not a "teacher" and does not speak to groups of people. David starts with an intriguing account of his own awakening. Readers have commented that although there is minimal question and answer format, David answers so many of the perplexing questions that arise in ordinary language but retaining the beauty and wonder of Liberation.

Perfect Brilliant Stillness

408 pages. *Isbn: 0-9547792-8-2 £13.25

"It is so rare to see any work that holds that essential and fundamental perception without compromise. Your book is a beacon which can shine through all of the fog and nonsense that is broadcast under the name of 'advaita' or 'non-duality'. Especially as that expression comes out of no-one!"

Tony Parsons author of *The Open Secret, All There Is* and *Nothing Being Everything*

"This book is a Gonzo Gita – a Gone-so Song of God; a soaring, rampaging loving outpouring of Unmanifest Source displayed in manifest consciousness, playing a complex spiritual melody through the hollow bamboo flute of a Vermont farmer/carpenter/building contractor who was all but ignorant of the non-dual tradition before a disorienting full enlightenment struck and he realized 'there's nobody home'."

Robert Gussner PhD, Professor Emeritus, University of Vermont Dept. of Religion

---

*UK edition only: US, Canada & rest of the world available from: www.nonduality.com/perfect_brilliant_stillness.htm

"The Self cannot be described but David Carse makes a very good effort. Quoting from Sufi and Taoist sages as well as Advaitin ones, he helps uncover the non-dual truth that is the essence of the phenomenal appearance. The language he uses is direct and carries the conviction of experience. In many books on Advaita there is the distinct feeling that what is said is in the realm of theory or based upon what has been read elsewhere; one is left in no doubt that this is not the case here. Although nothing new is being said, the material comes across so clearly, simply and self-evidently. And I think this is the key to why the book succeeds. The words carry the understanding to those seeking the explanations but they cannot prevent the heart-felt, mind-less, direct `knowing' from shining through and piercing the merely intellectual.

Although much is said about the inadequacy and ultimate failure of language to speak of reality, David's writing is very good. I have said in my own books that it is not possible to talk clearly about this subject without using the correct Sanskrit terminology but this book seems to give the lie to that statement. There are some very original metaphors and many brilliant, quotable observations. Sometimes, every other paragraph seems to contain a new profundity.

David is not a teacher of Advaita and specifically states that he does not teach. Beginners will probably not benefit and should perhaps look elsewhere to begin with. But, if you think you know it all already yet feel that `it' has still not clicked, this is definitely for you. It is the book for those who want to differentiate between intellectual understanding and realization. I have also noted that it seems to receive praise from both traditional and neo-Advaitins – and that is praise indeed!

I have mentioned elsewhere that I always pencil in the margins of any Advaita books that I read these days. Positive comments are marked: `good', `!' and Q (for `quote'); things that I don't understand are marked `?' or, if I disagree, `x'. There are very few `?', only a couple of x's and many Q's and good's. What more can I say? The only adverse comment that I would make – and it is a warning for potential readers as much as anything else – is that the early chapters do go on a bit! So, if you find that, don't be put off and give up; keep reading – it just gets better... and better!"

Dennis Waite author of *The Book of One* and *Back to the Truth*

In spiritual circles there is great value placed on personal growth, personal improvement, becoming a better person, becoming more aware, teaching others how to become better, making the world a better and more enlightened place. The hope for a better future, the belief in an upward spiritual evolution that carries the whole race with it, is like the belief that there is something wrong and something that needs to be done. It seems hard-wired into the human mechanism but is in fact the device by which the 'divine hypnosis' operates, keeping the dream characters motivated and occupied in the dream. This belief is an illusion, and it is what creates suffering.

In Truth, in the Absolute, in All That Is, there is no evolution, no progress, no becoming better, no becoming. All is as it is. The idea that the world is in bad shape and that the present point in history is pivotal and that something has to be done, is as old as the human mind; it has always seemed thus, at every point in 'human history.' In truth everything is in perfect balance; the world never gets better and never gets worse, although to the apparent individual instruments it may seem that it does.

Teachers who draw on these recurring themes in the dream to appeal to the ego's hopes and dreams and to popularize their message are deluding themselves and others and have not seen beyond the dream. This belief in ongoing evolution, the dream of becoming a better person, the goal of improving oneself and others and society and making the world a better place: all these and more certainly seem to be noble beliefs and goals by any standards. Our cultures value them as ideals and it is believed that these high goals are what keep individuals and the human race from descending or regressing into chaos. And of course it is the 'divine hypnosis' itself that allows these beliefs, because without them the dream would not go on.

But as Buddhist teacher Chogyam Trungpa Rinpoche has noted,

> *"Enlightenment is the great and final disappointment, the dissolution of all our egoic fantasies and grand hopes."*

This is true seeing, and it will never sell in the revival tents. What is being said here is not a politically correct message, or even a spiritually correct message. It is not a comforting message, and it will never in any culture be popular. It is only the truth, as near as can be told. All is as it is.

The ego seeks fulfillment, and if awakening is marketed as satisfying that need, then what is being offered is bogus. True awakening is awakening to the annihilation, the dissolution of that which seeks fulfillment.

> *"Transformative spirituality, authentic spirituality, is revolutionary. It does not legitimate the world, it breaks the world; it does not console the world, it shatters it. And it does not render the self content, it renders it undone."*
>
> (Ken Wilber)

And of course, as you may perhaps intuit at this point, the wonderful aching beauty is that in this annihilation every longing, hunger and thirst that any mind/body apparatus ever felt is resolved and dissolved, perfected, healed and made forever irrelevant. The ego seeks fulfillment, but what is Understood in this annihilation is so huge that no mind, no ego, no heart could ever possibly hold it. The human race has no idea what fulfillment truly is.

From *Perfect Brilliant Stillness*
Chap.27, p214; Confused Thinking

John Greven was born in 1961 in Oklahoma. At the age of eighteen he was struck by the idea that the "creator of the universe" couldn't be as limited as was taught. This began a search that took him through various religions, philosophies, metaphysics, and meditation. The search went on at various levels of intensity and commitment for 25 years. In 2004 a meeting with John Wheeler contributed to bringing the search to an abrupt end as the simple and obvious truth was seen. *Oneness* takes the reader step by step to the Unescapable Reality that is the Self.

Oneness: the Destination You Never Left*

92 pages. Isbn: 978-0-9551762-0-3 £7.50 / $10.95

Website
www.onenessjustthat.com

"This is a beautiful book. It is very simple, direct and to the point. It will be a benefit to many people.

I am very pleased that the message, which Nisargadatta Maharaj was a vehicle for, is being passed on. This lineage is influencing many and the message is continuing to spread throughout the world.

It is obvious that the author has investigated along the lines he points to in this book. He has dispersed the clouds of conceptual beliefs with basic clear seeing. This book, itself, is the proof that he knows whereof he speaks.

The book takes the seeker locked in the confusion of the mind to the immediacy of the Natural State.

Don't under-rate the obviousness and simplicity contained in this book and the search is over!"

"Sailor" Bob Adamson

---

*A Dutch translation of *Oneness*, *Eén*, is available from Samsara Publications, Holland.

"Reading your book this morning was "the missing link." Having tried "Who am I?" and not really understanding what the heck I was doing, only barely getting what it was pointing at, it finally "hits home" now. Another pointer and a powerful one, that book of yours. It is very tricky using words to describe the undescribable and I guess the most they can do is help to create a stopping or seeing through of the thoughts that have fooled you into thinking that they are you. Your book does this better than most for "me".

P.C.

"I read your book some time ago and I have been letting it sink in. Although the book itself is very brief, the depth is astonishing. You did indeed go beyond what other "nondual" books present. Nothing I have read or studied has come close to your clear exploration of "Who Am I". More importantly, fewer still have pointed at the Absolute state, which Nisargadatta states is prior to consciousness."

P.D.

"This book is a beautiful inquiry into 'Who am I?' with direct pointers at Transcendental Truth.

Questions are asked from many angles and we look at a simple pointing to the experience of reality, without the filter of the mind, to that which is common to all of us, that which the mind has overlooked. You drop the suffering of the separate ego by seeing your true nature as one with all beingness. You investigate the claims, beliefs and assumptions that the mind has told you. Upon examination of your beliefs, you see them effortlessly fall away, as those concepts are seen to be false.

I was left in a deep peace, "Once the conceptual 'I' is dropped by the mind as a valid center, then the door swings open to what is being pointed to, the emptiness that is full." You see "It is all just appearance within the source and the source is what you are."

This book provides a simple, in-depth analysis of self inquiry, with profound insights, stated with a wry wit and an unwavering pointing at Presence/Awareness as the Oneness that we are."

Amazon.com Reviewer

Presence of Awareness
Awareness of Presence

Look closely at these.
Who are you? Do you know?

The answer to the question seems to make more sense if it is asked: what are you? The answer is that you are the real. *You are the reality that gives validity to things.* You are the *unchanging reality* in which the temporal reality moves across and through. You are the constant in an ever changing appearance. *Every-thing* appears within spaceless awareness.

You are a presence, which cannot be defined by the mind. You are presence/awareness in which everything, including the mind appears.

Presence cannot be any more or less present than what it is. It is pristine, untouched, and undeniable, regardless of life's circumstances and the thoughts of the mind. Awareness cannot be any more or less aware than what it is while allowing everything to effortlessly appear across its surface. Presence of Awareness, Awareness of Presence – whole and complete, untouched by time, space, events, or thought. Everything that is, appears in awareness. Awareness does not pick, choose, or judge what appears upon or within it. It does not matter what happens, awareness contains it as it is.

The mind then gets involved and suddenly things appear as what you think about them, but *prior to, during, and after that,* awareness lovingly embraces all that is, including the lies about who you are. Even while the mind is rebelling against something, awareness shines its light on that rebellion. Some use the analogy of a mirror to describe awareness. It reflects *every-thing* clearly without being changed in any way by what it reflects.

You may think, "Okay, I am presence/awareness." Once you begin to look at this and take it into the mind – the mind will want to turn it into something that it has.

Adding that concept onto the "I" thought. "I am aware." "I am present." But, if that is what is happening, you're not "tuning in" so to speak to the actual presence/awareness that is readily available to be seen. Presence/awareness is not in the mind and it cannot be contained in the mind. The thought of presence/awareness, as with the rock, is not the actual. You don't have awareness; you are awareness. You don't have a presence; you are presence. The thought of it turns what you actually are into a concept to which the mind can relate. While that is happening, you are the presence/awareness standing in the clear waiting to be discovered. This cannot be stressed enough, *everything is just an appearance within the awareness that you are*; without exception, everything.

Only the thought of presence/awareness can be brought into the mind for consideration. While you are thinking about presence/awareness you are present and aware. You can't objectify what you are.

So how do you stay with the presence/awareness that you are? How do you "tune in"? It is effortless because it is always on... you don't have to try, just see. If you're trying, then you're just not noticing that it is inescapable and functioning all the time; or you're trying to become something that you already are! Presence is effortless. Awareness is effortless. The fact is you don't have any choice but to stay with it, because you are it! Presence does not change. Awareness does not change. It does not move. It does not hide. But be watchful: don't turn the obvious presence/awareness into a concept or an idea about yourself. Stay with the livingness of it by not following what the mind thinks about it. *Presence-Awareness is in the ever present now.*

Presence/awareness refer to the simple, undeniable beingness that is present and aware. In the same way that we have looked at presence/awareness - beingness *points* to that timeless, spaceless Self.

There was a recent question that began along the lines of, "When you take your attention within to see the beingness..."

This question points out a rather basic misunderstanding and hints at an expectation of what is being pointed to and where it is. There are numerous problems with the question, but really two often overlooked misunderstandings work together to complicate clear seeing. The first one is attention. Attention is a tool of the mind, like the hand is to the body; attention can only be placed on things. Attention is nothing more than the focus of the senses and mental ideas on an object. As we have discussed, what you are is not a thing that the mind can grasp. So, although it was never explicitly stated, let us be clear. Attention cannot be placed on what you are. Attention can be placed on the thoughts of presence and the thoughts of awareness, on thoughts of beingness, but not the actual beingness. This is a confusing point because the suggestion is there to "stay with" the presence/awareness that you are. Well, how is that done if not using attention? The truth is that you have no choice but to stay with the presence/awareness that you are, because it is what you are. The subtlety is to recognize, and specifically for the mind to recognize, that your beingness is always present whether attention is on the idea of being aware or being present - or not. There is literally nothing you can do to get out of your own beingness. So, attention is a tool of the mind and attention will never touch what you are - or what is being pointed to. Therefore, it is of no value in final understanding.

From Oneness
Chap.7, p.51; Presence/Awareness

Nathan Gill is a pioneering and influential voice in the world of contemporary advaita. In *Already Awake* he consistently points out that all prescriptions for escape from the drama of separation (the sense of the separate self) actually serve as its reinforcement. Also included by way of a preface to *Already Awake* is Nathan's autobiographical booklet, *Clarity*.

'Spiritual' dialogues usually aim to guide the seeker towards enlightenment, towards escape from identification as a suffering individual. In *Being: The Bottom Line,* however, Nathan Gill points out that 'enlightenment' only appears significant from the viewpoint of 'me' – it's only the story of 'me' that requires enlightenment.

Nathan was born in 1960 and lives in rural England.

Already Awake

162 pages. Isbn: 09547792-2 £10.80 / $19.73

Being: the bottom line:

120 pages. Isbn: 978-0-9551762-2-7 £8.40 / $12.00

Interviews:

Amigo No.4 (www.ods.nl/am1gos/)

This Is It, Jan Kersschot, Watkins Publishing, 2004

Website

www.nathangill.com

"Now it was seen that all of life is a great play. There is only ever knowing, but this knowing is seemingly veiled by the mesmerisation with the 'I' thought and all the other thoughts that appear as 'my' story. Our true nature as Consciousness is awareness and *the appearances. The 'I' is simply a part of the scenery, as are all the other various images, and when it is seen through – or seen for what it is – then seeking and tension fall naturally away."*

"Nathan Gill's book, Already Awake, was mind blowing in a beautiful, subtle life changing way. So much of what is termed Advaita and non-dual teaching (which I have been steeped in now for over 4 years) has an elitist aspect that directs people to follow various prescriptions to get somewhere, purportedly to what is real, beyond the illusions of ego. Previously, I was wholeheartedly into this approach. Nathan's book so clearly depicts what is so glaringly obvious, that if one is even in the least open to the fact that there can be no movement toward or away from what is, then a deep seeing is just about unavoidable. Ego identified or not, "awakeness" is not something distant and rare, but is all that is. This book puts this realization in the most simple and direct manner. There is not a trace of elitism or self-aggrandizement, whatsoever. There is a real, warm, open invitation to just see the obvious and to celebrate everything as the expression of the divine by the divine as the divine. Nothing and no one is excluded. So many teachings seem to place themselves above the so-called "ordinary" people. Nathan does anything but this with his words. The expression that comes through him is simply the humble beloved embracing, being all and everyone and everything and being no-thing and no one. I fell in love with what is, as it is, as I am and seem to be. This is miraculous and my gratitude is endless."

Amazon.com reviewer

"For even the most seasoned Advaita traveller, Nathan's book may be considered the 'end of the road'. With beautiful simplicity he puts to rest the hidden duality that seems to reside within even the most profound expressions of non-duality.

This allows spiritual seeking with all of it's inherent suffering to come to an end in a truly effortless way.

Nathan's book is clear, simple and profoundly complete. I consider it to be the highest expression of non-duality available in print."

Amazon.com reviewer

Questioner: Do you still have the sense of being a separate person?

Nathan: There isn't necessarily any sudden dropping of the 'I', but maybe the 'I' is seen through. Perhaps there is more of the remembering of our true nature and less of a sense of being located 'inside' a body; more of a sense of the body simply arising here along with everything else, and appearing as a viewing or experiencing centre – like our cells in the 'body of the one' analogy. When the thought story running simultaneously with this bodily appearance is seen through, then ease is revealed, the tension goes out of it all.

So is there still sometimes a forgetting for the character Nathan, then?

If Nathan describes in a concrete way what is the life of the character here, then within the play it appears to promote continued mesmerisation with the thought story – perhaps comparing the life of Nathan with 'my' life... Nathan maybe has something that 'I' don't, so therefore 'I' need to awaken, etc.

But Nathan is merely one image appearing amongst all the others. This is all the appearance of oneness, as these images, and it just happens that the Nathan image seems to have the function of appearing in the play to point out that there is no awakening – there is only already awakeness.

But for the character Nathan there must have been a story of all this unfolding. Can you describe how that happened?

Well, when we focus on the character Nathan – that there was a point where the character Nathan realised something or changed in some way – then already there is involvement with the thought story, a projection into past. And this appears to support the thought story, the assumption of 'I', and the idea that 'I' will realise or recognise what Nathan has recognised 'in the future'. This is the way the thought story is supported within the play.

Whereas this little scene in the play appears to be about the undermining – the seeing through – of the story.

Presence is easily overlooked if Nathan starts harping on about some event, some point in time when there was realisation. All that encourages the mesmerisation with the thought story. In fact there is simply the registering of all that presently appears. Nothing else is happening.

Everything is just happening?

Yes.

It's as insubstantial as a dream at night?

Yes, but with this daytime dream, there is no waking up out of the dream. What we are referring to as the recognition of our true nature as oneness is waking *into* the dream.

So Nathan at one stage was in a forgetting ...

No, no, there was never Nathan at a 'stage' – there is only the present appearance of Nathan.

'Nathan at a stage' is a story?

Yes, Nathan at some stage – 'when something happened' – is a story, a story arising presently.

Nathan is a picture appearing now, and the history of Nathan is the thought story appearing now, just for entertainment in the dream?

Yes, all there is presently of Nathan is an image appearing at the front of the room.

What gymnastics we do with thought forms!

'We' don't do anything with thought forms.

Why can't we just remain in the maya and enjoy the show?

Yes, if there is identification as the character, mesmerisation, and the character has a yacht in the bay and a few million in the bank, sunny days, happy families, the good life – then yes, mesmerisation is absolutely fine! (*laughter*)

But when you get really ill or something, then you go back to seeking.

There is seeking to get out of the play. All the while the play is going well, then all seems absolutely fine.

But what does it matter if one thinks like that anyway?

'One' isn't thinking like that – it's all happening as a story, as a play. But yes, there is no point to seeking and recognising. There is no more point or 'special-ness' to this scene in the play, with the story of seeking and recognising our true nature, than there is to any other scene of 'ordinary' life, or seeking for material happiness, etc.

So why are we trying to see then?

'We' aren't trying to see anything – this struggle to see is happening as a scene in the play.

From *Already Awake*
Kensington, London; Afternoon Talk; p.56

Guy Smith: This is Unimaginable and Unavoidable: Irresponsible writings on non-duality does not play into the hands of convention or popular concepts about enlightenment. Consisting of prose pieces, autobiographical confessions, poems and 'notices' it challenges every assumption and concept that you may have ever held about spirituality.

The narrator or `voice' is nowhere to pin down and is expansive and unpredictable as the weather. Beautifully fresh, exhilarating and timelessly alive.

This is Unimaginable and Unavoidable

284 pages. Isbn: 0-9547792-5-8 £11.25 / $17.95

Interview

Amigo No.10 (www.ods.nl/am1gos)

"So there would be this traveling to these meetings ... and fantasies would come up about being on a really special, exciting, esoteric adventure – being involved in something terribly rarified and superior. And of course, with this was the hope that 'when I get there – there will be this wonderful epiphany ... some majestic blossoming ... all the exact kind of riches thought dreams up and longs for!' And then I'd hear 'there is only oneness ... you needn't have come here' – and there would be this painful disappointment ... at not having found what I wanted: the sense of being let down.

This really is the only kind of message that gets to the heart of the matter. It rips the dream to shreds. Any sense of path, progress, improvement, direction, motion – can only be pure dream. It is the sense that there is a divisible reality of multiple separate things: better and worse; here and there; enlightened and asleep. So really, I followed no path before realisation ... and whenever I believed I was going somewhere, this delusion was abruptly dispelled by the message: 'there is nowhere to go'."

"I like this book a lot. The style of writing and expression is lively, fun, intelligent, joyous, radical, strong, vulnerable, outrageous, ordinary. It's about nonduality, sex, politics, movies, meditation, sex, pop music, science, art, enlightenment, sex, and pre-enlightenment experience, and more. Mostly it's a compilation of intelligent and sparkling writings on nonduality.

The writings are unstructured. Each chapter is brief, one to four pages. The author could have included the writings on sex, pre-enlightenment, and nondual perspectives, for example, in separate chapters or sections, but instead he scattered them throughout the book. The author explains: "This text is best treated like a treasure-chest filled with diamonds, as opposed to, say, a treasure map." It's an effective way to present the material since it corresponds to what is: 'this is.' ."

Jerry Katz author of *One: Essential Writings on Nonduality*

"I love this book! It is passionate, uncompromising, irreverent, intimately openhanded and wonderfully without any sense of order or progression.

Throughout the whole work there is very little that the cunning guru mind can get hold of and turn into a belief system. There is a powerful invitation within these outpourings which seems to harbour and generate a feeling of the sensuous, the impersonal, the unbounded mystery that lies beyond the words.

This is not a book to wade through steadily, but rather a deep pool in which to dip one's foot . . . and maybe fall in.

There is a proliferation of so-called Advaita/Non-dual literature available today, and virtually all of it is borne out of a fundamental misconception about the nature of being. However, during the last decade some rare, clear voices have emerged out of the mist, and Guy's work is surely an inspiring and unique confirmation of this wonderful message."

Tony Parsons author of *The Open Secret, All There Is* and *Nothing Being Everything*

"Nondual expression is very often contradictory. One says 'When awakening happens...' one moment, and the next moment one says 'there is no awakening; all there is is awakeness'. One says 'there is no time' and then, 'Four months ago, when it first became apparent that there was no time'!! One says, "There is no space, no such thing as space" and then one says 'And that is seen 'over here', while that same seeing is overlaid by beliefs "over there". One says, 'There is the appearance of colours and forms' and one says, 'There is no colour, no form, nothing'. One says, 'There is no one here', and then one says, 'Today when I was going to the shops to buy some eggs...' This contradiction happens only because words describe the limited. Words describe something located somewhere. Even if the word is 'everything' there is a tendency for the mind to make an abstraction of this, cognising a symbol or a structure or a movement or an image that is supposed to represent 'everything'. So attempting to talk about nonduality is a bit like dancing on hot coals. Everywhere you tread, each word you choose, each phrase, each subject, is dangerous, is misleading, is conducive to perpetuating the idea of separative selfhood and all its difficulties and hurtfulness. One dances on coals; one dances to keep moving away from words, to keep eluding thought, while at the same time, leaping right onto fresh problems, fresh structures.

Having said all this, there are ways in which words are wonderfully expressive of nonduality.

From *This is Unimaginable and Unavoidable*
Chap.89, P.174; Nondual expression is contradictory

A friend of mine sees a teacher who advocates technique. And this friend says to me, 'I don't see why technique necessarily enforces the sense of 'me'. I cannot argue with him, because, in a way, there is no reason why technique must generate the sense of a 'me'. The fact is technique simply happens, appears in consciousness, or doesn't. This may or may not be accompanied by the belief that there is someone there instigating the occurrence. So meditation and so forth is absolutely fine, immaculate, and this teaching here does not discourage it. Funnily enough, and all the same, this passage finds itself moving towards a natural critique of technique. This teaching does not discourage method the same way it doesn't encourage it. And the reason this is happening is that it is the sense that something needs to be done, whether that be to start meditating or stop, that engenders the erroneous belief that enlightenment is somewhere else, that there is something, a me, that isn't yet enlightened. There is no 'me' and there is only enlightenment. In a way, technique *is* being discouraged here, but only in the sense that not practising a method is a subtle way of practising the method of not practising, all of which tends to foster the blinding propaganda of enlightenment: that there is such a thing, that some people have it, and one day I might too. Technique can also encourage the topsy-turvy sense of 'I am experiencing oneness'. One often hears 'masters' saying 'move into this', 'play with this', 'stay with this' and 'be with this'. The whole thrust of this is highly misleading and just plain mistaken. It is far more helpful to say that 'this', oneness, experiences being you, or at least experiences what is being experienced, that may include a sense of 'self' (that is the product of misinformation). The source appears as the appearance. Seeing things 'this way round' is a far more helpful and potent pointer to seeing the nature of reality. The actual raw fact, however, is that the source and appearance are the same oneness; there is no hierarchy, no difference, no 'way round'. To suggest that one can 'be' or 'not be' 'with this', this oneness, is just daft; that which is imagined to be 'not with this' is actually wholly and solely 'this' itself.

From *This is Unimaginable and Unavoidable* P.175

Joan Tollifson: Skillfully written, *Awake in the Heartland* offers the non-dual understanding and direct approach of Advaita and Zen, grounded in the actuality of daily life with all its messiness, complexity, uncertainty, paradox, and apparent imperfection. Joan reveals her own life with candid honesty, demolishing all ideas of how things "should" be.

If there seems to be a gap between what the enlightenment books describe and what you find in your own life, if you still think enlightenment is something that will happen to you in the future (or not at all), if you're still chasing exotic experiences or self-improvement or some final breakthrough, then this book may be just what you need to wake up to the truth that what you are seeking is already here.

Awake in the Heartland

264 pages. Isbn: 978-0-9551762-4-1 £10.80 / $19.95

Interview

Amigo No.7 (www.ods.nl/am1gos/)

Website

www.joantollifson.com

"I realized this whole quest for self-perfection (and personal enlightenment) was a movie, a dream. The movie was absolutely perfect, just the way it was. It was a great movie! But it was a movie. Nothing about Joan needed to change. No Big Bang was needed. It was a revelation to see that Joan's whole effort to wake up from the movie was nothing more than another part of the movie. The awakening that was so desperately being sought had in fact never been absent. But this awakening was not an experience to be had (for any experience would just be another scene in another movie), and it did not happen to Joan, for how can a mirage wake up from a mirage?"

"In this lovely book, Joan says that "every moment is a kiss." Every time I open and read a passage from *Awake in the Heartland*, I feel that I have been kissed by this sense of immediate presence. Thank you, Joan, for this precious gift."

Josh Baran, 365 nirvana here and now

"There is a vibrant energy that emanates from the pages of this book that cannot help but resonate with and stir the same essence in the reader and awaken them to the ecstasy of what is – their own true nature. Because the personal story is so beautifully interwoven, the book answers the question so often asked by seekers: "Yes, I understand BUT... how do I live my life?" Joan is constantly showing the reader, by personal example, that life lives itself as IS no matter WHAT appears. I recommend it."

Sailor Bob Adamson

"An excellent book. Joan has a gift for writing clearly. Her willingness to share her own very human story points out the ordinariness of realization and how things just continue on as they do ... both before and after awakening."

Chuck Hillig, Enlightenment for Beginners,
The Way It Is, and Seeds for the Soul

"I can honestly say that of all the books I have read over the last twenty years (including all of those in your bibliography) this is simply the best and most honest treatment of the mysterious "enlightenment" topic ever. I thank you so much. Your treatment of issues such as 9/11 and the war and politics in relation to the whole "spiritual" or "enlightenment" thing is just the first time I have seen anyone even try to include all of that. So essential and so necessary. Great."

Ian McBain, a reader in Hong Kong

Finding the Absolute in the Relative

I have come to feel a deep love for our so-called humanness. The urge to transcend it completely, to leave Joan out of this book and write only the" purist" truth, has given way to a deeper truth which includes every-thing, even Joan! And that turns out to be the cosmic joke: the pure book wanted to write, the one that spoke only the absolute truth, is actually this book. There is no other book. This is the purity. This is the absolute. Finger-biting, stormy weather, heat, cold, sun, rain - white gulls flashing past my window, a dazzling moment of beauty, gone in an instant.

Everything is God

The first leaf on the tree outside my window has turned bright yellow. Other trees in the neighbourhood are starting to turn. It is raining and cooler. Fall is in the air. I've been in Chicago for a year now. It's the first year in decades that I have not left home and travelled somewhere else. Something has settled. I always imagined myself "settling" in some quiet, spacious, rural place, something more like Springwater. And here I am in Chicago, a big, noisy, polluted city, the last place I imagined myself. And yet, it is so deeply right, at least for right now. Everything in my life seems perfect: the years of getting drunk and stoned, the years of political activism, the years of meditation, the years in satsang. No one part seems any more holy than any other. It could not be otherwise. It's as if, for so many years I've been seeking salvation, and it suddenly dawns on me that there is no need of any such thing. There is no one to save. Nothing means anything; it all just is. And that isn't depressing. It's all "meaningless" the way a dance or a flower is mean-ingless. It doesn't need any meaning. Sometimes everything glows with beauty and light. Sometimes every-thing seems flat. Sometimes there is vast space. Sometimes there are thoughts. Sometimes there is contraction. Sometimes there is expansion.

I'm not chasing any particular state, trying to get it to endure forever. Experiences of all kinds arise. They pass. Somehow, in its raw ordinariness, Chicago is the perfect ground to recognize the obvious: What is, is. It really is that simple. Most remarkable of all, I've noticed that I don't want to finish first anymore in the Spiritual Race to the Imaginary Finish Line. The race has dissolved into thin air. The beauty of writing a book is that you don't know what it's about until it's over. It's like watching a photograph slowly appear in the developing tray. At first just a few amorphous shapes, and then slowly, out of nowhere, a coherent picture emerges. And it's all a magic trick, like the photograph. It's just an image inside an image inside an image, a photograph of nothing at all. At night there is heat lightning, the sky lighting up and flashing, the cicadas buzzing at a frenzied volume doing their bhajans. Walking in the morning, I see green leaves shimmering with light. Fruit hangs in the trees. I stand at an intersection, waiting to cross the street. A big truck rumbles past me, leaving a huge cloud of smelly exhaust. The exhaust is the Beloved just as much as the shimmering leaves. It's all beautiful. It's all God. I'm home.

From *Awake in the Heartland*
Chap.5, p.90; Everything is Grace

Richard Sylvester is a humanistic psychologist, therapist and lecturer. For thirty years he engaged with a variety of "spiritual practices" while also training in psychotherapeutic techniques and teaching counselling. In 2002 Richard met Tony Parsons and, as he writes in *I Hope You Die Soon*, "that was the end of what I thought had been my life". There then occurred two events which he describes in his book as 'awakening' and 'liberation'. Richard lives in a country town in South East England. He holds meetings about non-duality in London and other locations in the U.K.

I Hope You Die Soon*

120 pages. Isbn: 978-0-9551762-1-0 £8.00 / $12.00

Website

www.richardsylvester.com

---

* A German language translation, *Erleuchtet – und was Jetzt?*, is published by Random House Bertlesmann.

"What happens when searching ends is simply that searching ends. We could say that the person ends, the person dies. That's quite a dramatic way of putting it but it has a certain accuracy about it. But there is still a character and also feelings, preferences, likes and dislikes. It is just that these are seen no longer to belong to anyone. So rather than there being a person who gets angry, it's seen that anger simply arises. Rather than there being a person who likes coffee and doesn't like tea, it's now seen that a liking for coffee and a dislike of tea arises, but for no one."

"Richard's description of what has been seen in liberation is both eloquent and down to earth. His direct, uncluttered and concise expression can be readily identified with and speaks directly to that knowing which is beyond seeking."

Tony Parsons author of *The Open Secret, All There Is* and *Nothing Being Everything*

"I can't tell you how very enjoyable it was to read something so..... exquisitely phrased! You certainly have forthrightly "nailed" the subject powerfully. I would have to call you a "21st century replica of Wei Wu Wei". Thank you, most gratefully."

C.F. United States

"God, it's all so true! I have been "searching" for what feels like eons now! Yet your web page is the closest thing I have felt to the truth that I have ever read in my life."

C.M. United Kingdom

"Hopefully, this will be the last book you ever read. Richard Sylvester (may he rest in peace) has done an outstanding job of writing about This that is beyond all words, thoughts and imagination. Somehow, mysteriously, certain apparent writers are actually able to invite the apparent reader into the absolute freedom of liberation from the illusion of a separate self. YOU sit down to read this book and by the time it is finished, so are YOU! What a relief!"

Amazon Reviewer

Within the story, a year after awakening, I am standing in a shop in an ordinary country town. Suddenly but with great gentleness the ordinary is displaced by the extraordinary. The person again disappears completely and now it is seen clearly that awareness is everywhere and everything. The localised sense of self is revealed to be just an appearance. There is no location, no here or there. There is only oneness appearing as everything and this is what 'I' really am. 'I' am the shop, the people, the counter, the walls and the space in which everything appears. When the self disappears, and awareness is seen as everything, then this is seen for what it is, a wonderful hologram sustained by love.

At a certain time as a child, awareness appears to coagulate into a discrete space, becoming solid and separate from everything else. This is what creates the sense of 'me' with its hopes and fears and loves and burdensome responsibilities. The thoughts and feelings and sensory phenomena, which really simply arise in awareness, are now owned by someone, are now felt to belong to 'me'. And so the drama of being a person starts.

There is no locality to awareness other than 'everywhere'. There is only liberation. But in liberation the sense that 'I' am not liberated can and does arise. It manifests as the sense of separation, of being located over here rather than over there, separate from all other people and things. It brings fear, longing and hope, and it is highly addictive. It cannot see through itself and it may simply continue for seventy or eighty years until it ends at death. Or it may end sooner, anywhere, at any time.

Liberation is freedom from the burden of being a person who apparently has to make choices and decisions; choices and decisions which have consequences. What a wonderful relief it is to see that there is no choice, no person, no separation. Nothing you have ever done has ever led to anything because you have never done anything. No one has ever done anything although it appears that things have been done.

Isn't it wonderful that you have never made a choice in your life? There is nothing to regret, nothing to feel guilty about. Nothing could ever have been any different, nothing could ever have been any other way. Isn't that a relief? Nothing matters. There is nowhere to go. There is nothing that has to be done. There is no meaning and no morality. There is no help and no hope. You can let it all go, you can release all the tension. You can begin to enjoy the wonder of hopelessness and the gift of meaninglessness. You can begin to enjoy your complete helplessness.

In liberation it is seen that nothing has any meaning, it is simply what it is. The story does not stop. The story continues but now it is seen that it is just a story. All the passions of your apparent life are *just stuff happening*. The conflicts, the loves, the struggles for control and power, the victories and defeats are simply phenomena arising in oneness and falling away again with no meaning at all. Nothing has any more significance than anything else or could ever be greater or lesser. The Trojan war and a glass of beer are equal.

Except, of course, to the mind.

From *I Hope You Die Soon*
Chap.3, p.23; Liberation: Seeing 'I' am Everything

John Wheeler has risen to prominence as one of the most popular and clear communicators of self-enquiry in the style of his teacher, 'Sailor' Bob Adamson. His first meeting with 'Sailor' Bob is outlined in the following extract from *Awakening to the Natural State*.

The four books by John contain short autobiographical pieces and extensive correspondence with students. His most recent release, *You Were Never Born* (February 2007) contains an extended interview with John and a chapter of prose pieces.

Awakening to the Natural State

256 pages. Isbn: 0-9547792-3-1 £11.45 / $19.95

Shining in Plain View

272 pages. Isbn: 0-9547792-6-6 £11.45 / $19.95

Right Here, Right Now

308 pages. Isbn: 978-0-9551762-3-4 £11.45 / $19.95

You Were Never Born

276 pages. Isbn: 978-09553999-2-3 £11.45 / $19.95

Website
http://thenaturalstate.org/

"Prior to this understanding, we live in identification with whatever the mind conceives and presents to us about our identity. But the assumptions were based on a false understanding. This, in turn, was the basis of our suffering and problems. By re-looking at the whole picture afresh, we come to a clear and simple recognition of what we actually are, as opposed to what we think we are. This directly clears up the confusion and restores us to our natural state, our true condition."

"I met John Wheeler at a talk and book-signing event in the summer of 2005. The funny thing was, he wasn't really peddling his book very hard, and as the talk went on, I understood why not – John's whole message is that you don't need another book. So that was my introduction to unique thing #1 about John Wheeler: he's about pointing right at the simplicity of Being, not selling books or anything else. Just showing you the way - clearly, patiently, and as some would say, relentlessly.

Unique thing #2 about John Wheeler is that he looks like he could be the guy at the next desk in the office – no flowing garb, no eccentric hairstyle, no etheric gaze – and, there's no fuss along with his presentation – no request for silence before he enters the room, no bell-ringing, no photos of gurus on the wall. He's just a regular working guy, and the reason I mention this is that it was this very quality that instantaneously brought his message into focus for me – for the first time in my life, I realized this business is for regular people like you and me.

But I'm not saying being with John "felt" like being with the guy next door - far from it. The total clarity of his presence somehow knocked all the thoughts right out of my head (Unique thing #3). I sat in that room listening to people ask John questions, and I was sort of dazed, grinning, and thinking, what do these people think they have to find out? Can't they see there's nothing more to know - that they are already what they're looking for?

The reason I'm making this book review so personal is to tell you that I know first-hand, John Wheeler is the real deal. You can completely trust what he says, and his pointers are very clear...

....What John talks about in "Awakening to the Natural State" is not theoretical or metaphysical - he doesn't ask you to take anything on faith, but instead asks you to look and see for yourself (Unique thing #4). John continually shows you what direction to look and what kind of inquiry will assist you. His whole point as a teacher is to take you beyond the need for further help. And this he does directly and swiftly, by illustrating the utter simplicity of what we make such a muddle of in our heads.

Not just "highly recommended" – more than that! John Wheeler could end your search. Don't pass up this opportunity."

Annette Nibley

At one point, I met some Ramana Maharshi followers who had been on the path of self-inquiry for twenty or thirty years (and still working at it, I might add!). I was nowhere near their level of devotion, so it was pretty much out the picture that that approach would work for me. As I look at this now, it is not so much Ramana's teaching that is at fault, but the mind's inevitable tendency to turn any teaching into a practice. Practices, as I eventually learned, usually are interminable. This is because they are often based on false premises.

Intuitively, I felt that it was important for me to meet someone who had realized their true nature, someone whom I could trust, someone whom I could talk with in order to share my doubts and concerns. However, I was unsure which teachers were authentic; none seemed to resonate fully. I used to read Nisargadatta Maharaj's dialogues frequently. I could not understand his teaching fully, given all the Hindu verbiage and translation issues (he originally spoke in Marathi), but I felt intuitively that he was a free being. Many spiritual seekers, through reading his words, can sense the genuineness of his realization, even if they do not always experience everything he talks about. I used to wonder if there was anyone still living who had met Nisargadatta Maharaj and had really got the experience of self-knowledge. After all those years of searching, I eventually stumbled across Bob Adamson. Something resonated strongly. Even when I read the pages on his website, there was a strong feeling of 'maybe this is it'.

Just prior to discovering Bob Adamson, I had a vivid dream of Nisargadatta Maharaj, in which he was encouraging me not to give up the search for spiritual understanding. Shortly afterwards, I learned about Bob Adamson. Not wanting to miss the chance of meeting an authentic teacher (having missed the chance to see Nisargadatta Maharaj while he was alive), I decided to visit Bob in person in Australia. You can imagine my motivation (or perhaps desperation!) in going to Australia on the chance that he might be able to clarify my doubts and questions.

What I have found is that the understanding of our true nature almost never comes from reading books or thinking about it. The best books are primarily the records of dialogues that took place between a seeker and a teacher at some point in the past. In reading such books, we are trying to understand an experience that took place in the past (through words and concepts on the page). A book is like a map pointing to something real that was experienced in a dialogue between living people. Usually, we do not have a clear understanding of what is being revealed (at least I didn't) and we are trying to figure it out in the mind. This is a noble attempt, but as Bob Adamson pointed out within a few minutes of talking to him, 'The answer can never be found in the mind'. The experience of spiritual understanding and freedom is not forthcoming, so we naturally assume that we are not 'there' (wherever 'there' is). We think there must be some technique or path involved to get there. But somehow we are not quite sure what it is! The result is that the mind keeps generating the same old bondage and suffering. This is a frustrating cycle, because we intuitively feel a glimmer of light or truth in the readings, but the actual experience eludes us. The majority of seekers that I have met have had a similar experience. Many are driven to try to find a living teacher, in order to get some guidance and assistance on the spiritual path. This was what happened for me.

I met many teachers, but it wasn't until I met Bob Adamson that I was convinced that I was dealing with someone who had fully realized his true nature. Something radically shifted for me because I came face-to-face with the vitality, the confidence, the energy of that understanding. It was a remarkable experience and quite different from anything I had encountered in my years of seeking. The first day after I arrived, we had a chance to meet and talk. As we sat together, he looked me in the eyes and said point blank, 'Do you have any doubts or questions? Is there anything you need to know?' It was somewhat disarming because I realized he was free of doubts and was essentially offering me a chance to have the same experience for myself right then and there. The implication, it seemed to me, was 'The seeking is over, the reading is over. You are here. Are you ready to go for this completely here and now?' Fortunately, I jumped at the chance. I cast aside my theoretical knowledge and got down to getting off my chest my real doubts, questions and problems.

From *Awakening to the Natural State*
Chap 1, P.13; Meeting 'Sailor' Bob Adamson

Question: I have practised Zen for thirty years with Japanese or European masters in Riutakudji, Tokyo, Paris and London. I have gone through some koans. But I must say that in reading some of your articles recently I have realized with clearness and an unaccustomed intensity what is meant by no-separation, egoless and emptiness. You have unearthed the inner being which is this intimate yet universal presence we are invited to contemplate and then be during Zazen meditation and afterwards. How many have been the long hours and days of meditation (and, I dare say, suffering!) until now. Your words made a real breakthrough. My first master told me, 'Kill Jim!' (my name). You can see here the typical 'brutality' of Zen! But I insist – never had the absence of 'Jim' been so clearly and easily perceived than in reading your conversations. Of course, the 'I' is yet lurking behind the door. That is why I want to ask if you could send me a word (or two) to help in this seeing of the natural state (which I presume is the same as the 'Buddha Nature', as they call it in Zen)?

John: All that I can say is that the presence of awareness which is with you right now, that simple sense of existence which is brightly aware, is your true nature. It needs no attainment because it is fully and clearly present. Awakening and enlightenment are at best concepts attempting to point to the ever-awake and clear presence that you are. Once understood, no awakening is called for. It is the recognition of your natural state, which has been present all along, but perhaps unnoticed. We search and meditate as long as we are not clear that what we are seeking we already are. What you are is not a limited entity, but the clear, knowing-presence in which all appearances rise and set. Know this and be at peace. All the imagined problems and doubts fall to pieces when you see this. There is no one left to have problems. There is only open, clear, spacious presence-awareness.

From *Right Here, Right Now*
Chap 55. P. 154; No One Left to Have Problems

'Sailor' Bob Adamson: In 1976 on a visit to the Ashram of Swami Muktananda in Ganeshpuri, near Bombay, Bob Adamson was introduced to Sri Nisargadatta Maharaj. His message struck home and for the past 30 years 'Sailor' Bob has shared this understanding with seekers from around the world who visit him at his home in Melbourne, Australia. His style is direct and simple, a guided enquiry into the true Self.

What's Wrong with Right Now?

148 pages. Isbn: 0-9547792-0-7 £10.25 / 18.00

Presence-Awareness: Just This and Nothing Else

148pages. Isbn: 0-9547792-4-X £9.25 /$ 16.50

Interview

Living Reality: My Extraordinary Summer with 'Sailor' Bob Adamson.
James Braha, Hermetician Press, 2006

The Advaita Show: http://advaita.thepodcastnetwork.com

Website

http://members.iinet.net.au/~adamson7/

"Everything comes from, appears in, and returns to this natural emptiness. The coming and going of things is transience, but the cognising emptiness, being empty, does not come and go. Being empty, it is of itself no thing. It can never be filled or emptied of things, for things appearing in emptiness have no independent nature of themselves, and so in reality things are the same emptiness appearing as other. Every thing perceived is emptiness."

"Bob Adamson is an Australian who ended his spiritual search in 1976 in the presence of the renowned Sri Nisargadatta Maharaj. Ever since, he has been helping others to end their search. When he says that he abides as That, it is a bold but convincing statement. Although the themes in this collection of talks about nonduality are conventional and expected, the sense of living truth pouring out of them has nothing to do with certainty of ideas, but everything to do with his certainty of Being. Being is the foundation, the starting point and the ending point of his teaching. Abiding as That, Adamson speaks with the authority, the force and the immediacy of truth...

The title of the book summarizes his teaching: problems exist in the mind only, not in the here and now. That is a familiar teaching in nonduality. But, as Adamson's students know, his approach to it is penetratingly direct and immediate. He insists on remaining in the present, just as is. Noticeably absent from his talks is any mention of enlightenment, or awakening, or any implication of a future goal to be reached. His point is: you're already there; you're already complete; you're already eternally present as Awareness. To see that you're already free, all that's required is understanding.

....Not everyone, of course, will respond to his message or to his direct mode of delivery, just as not everyone has responded to Nisargadatta's or to Ramana Maharshi's. Not everyone hears what is actually said without colouring it according to their own beliefs. It's that familiar question of ripeness. As measured by the responses of students at the talks, it's apparent that Adamson's words sail right over the heads of some. No matter. For them, this is still beneficial preparatory instruction. But it's also apparent that the same words pierce the hearts of other students and profoundly transform them. For those who are ready, this can be the fast track to understanding".

Dennis Trunk, 3rd Millennium Gateway (www.thirdmg.com)

Let's look again at the analogy of the iron in the fire. We put the iron in the fire. It will become red like the fire. It will become hot like the fire. If you grasp it, it will burn you like the fire. It takes on the attributes of the fire. Now, take it out of the fire, what will it do? Will it get red? Will it burn? It has no substance of its own. It has no power to do these things, to be red hot, to burn. It has no power of its own to do these things.

The same with this idea that I have about myself. If it wasn't for that pure intelligence in the background, I couldn't have a single thought. It can't stand on its own. Another way of putting it is each one of you is seeing right now. You are hearing right now. Is that so? Tell me, does the ear say, 'I hear'? Or does the eye say, 'I see'? Does the backside sitting on the seat say, 'I feel'?

What says, 'I see', 'I hear', 'I feel'? Doesn't a thought come up translating what is happening as 'I see' or 'I hear'? Look at it from another angle. Does the idea in the mind 'I see' actually see? Does the idea in the mind 'I hear', hear? Or does the idea in the mind 'I feel', does that feel?

Q: No.

The thought comes up after the seeing, after the hearing. It is all happening prior to the thinking, just as it is. So, you can see from that, it's like the piece of iron. It has taken on the attributes of that pure intelligence, which is registering everything as it is, and believes itself to have the power.

You can see from that, that added to this image of myself, it believes it has personal volition, personal power. In addition, it needs a God or something else to make it whole because things are not going the way it expects them to. If it had such power why are things not going the way it wants it to, if it is running the show? The unlimited potential has limited itself into the shape or form of a poor miserable human being. And we live from that point until we see that we were never that.

All these pointers you will see when you start to question. You will see clearly that this idea or image that I have about myself is not what I really am at all. It is an idea based on past events and experiences. Not only does it have no reality as such, but it's a dead image. It is based on yesterday, yesterday's events and happenings. There is no livingness in it whatsoever. As it appears and comes up, it comes up presently. Like the piece of iron in the fire, it is in the fire and heated by the fire. And so it is with the intelligence. The intelligence is heating up this idea, this image, and it believes itself to have the power. But it never did have!

In seeing that there is no centre here, then I'm free from that seeming bondage. The cage that I have built around myself, the cage of limitations, is that I believe myself to be a separate entity, a person, an individual. As soon as that idea of separation comes, there is immediate insecurity, immediate vulnerability and the anxieties, fears, resentments, self-pity. And everything else must come from that image of separation, because it is trying to make itself whole or complete. You are the timeless! Thought is time appearing on the timeless.

Looking from the other angle, right here, right now, everyone is breathing; everyone's heart is beating; blood is coursing around the body; hair is growing; fingernails are growing; cells are being replaced; food is being digested. Who is making any effort to do it? Is there any 'me' or idea in the mind saying, 'I have to take the next breath', 'I've got to beat my heart', 'I have to digest my food'? Or is it happening effortlessly? Is there an innate intrinsic intelligence, an energy within that manifestation of the body that is coursing the blood through your veins right now? Isn't it causing the diaphragm to draw down, bringing in the air, then pushing it up to expel the air? It is taking all the food and all these various things that are needed to these different cells.

You can feel that energy. You can feel it in your fingertips and in your toes, if you like to watch closely enough, to feel closely enough. You can feel it there, pulsating, throbbing. The livingness is pulsing and throbbing through this pattern of energy right now. Effortlessly. No one is making an effort to do it. It is even causing the thinking. That energy has to find outlets. It shines out of your eyes as the light by which you see the world. What effort are you making to see? What effort are you making for that light to be in your eyes? What effort to hear? That intelligence, that innate, intrinsic intelligence, which pulsates through this body, is registering everything, right here, right now, just as it is. There is a direct experience of this, right now. Just like a mirror reflects everything just as it is. Or like a camera takes a photograph, just as it is. You are hearing the cars going by. You are seeing the movements in this room, smelling any odors that are present. All is registered just as it is and I mean just as it is. It is uncorrected, unmodified, unaltered, just purely and simply, as is.

The mind names things. There are gaps in the thoughts continually where it is starting and stopping within you. Seeing and knowing that, those gaps become longer. The seeing and the hearing can and do happen without the naming, just being registered as is.

It is not the nature of the mind to be simple. It will go on analysing - analysis paralysis - creating all sorts of stories just to perpetuate itself. The mind will come up and try to modify what is. It will try and correct it or alter it. 'I don't like this'. 'This is good'. 'This is bad'. Then there is a resistance to what is. The mind is translating what is being registered. You don't have to look very hard to see that any resistance is conflict.

So, the idea that 'I don't like this' is just an idea in the mind. What is it that I don't like? I don't like the chair or the table. How do I know that it's a chair or a table? I have named it from some previous experience. I'm no longer with what is. I'm with the name. The name I've given it is just another idea in the mind. So, the mind is in conflict with itself, a seeming energy blockage, a resistance to what is.

If it is just what is and there is no resistance to it,

what is happening? There's no conflict there whatsoever and things just express as is. That doesn't mean you have to sit down and do something. Everything will be done, as is. But if the resistance comes up and 'I don't like this', then what happens? That thought gets hold of it and builds it up and builds it up and builds it up. So what starts off as a little resentment will build up until the energy will be such that it has to be acted on. It will come out as some activity, anger, violence or whatever

This is where all 'my' problems arise from, from that dualism of 'me' and the 'other'. That sense of separation, that insecurity, that 'me' fears the unknown. Because that 'me' is the separation, it constantly fears. It would rather stay in the old way, no matter how unpleasant it is. 'I'll stay here rather than step out into the unknown'. Take that step into the unknown, into the no thing and see! An old saying is, 'Do the thing you fear and the death of fear is certain.' Let the intuitive take over without the 'me' thinking it knows better.

So, I understand there is no 'me' from this point of view. It has been seen clearly. Then I also understand that there can be no 'you' as such either. So, if there is no 'me' and there is no 'you', who is superior? Or who is inferior? What would I want of yours?

From *What's Wrong with Right Now?*
Chap.4, p.52

Bob: When you realize that you never find an answer to it in the mind, what happens? Without trying to do anything, that sense of looking there sort of drops away. When that drops away, the energy of beliefs is not going into all this thinking. That energy is there to be utilized in the moment. It makes a big difference.

Q: It is incredibly freeing.

Bob: Yes. We always thought and believed that we were going to work it out sooner or later in the mind. That constant struggle, that constant dissipation of energy is happening. No matter how hard we look there, we will never find the answer because the mind can't contain it. The mind, being a thing, can't grasp or contain no thing. So, what is the point in looking? Full stop. Like the questioner and the question, when you see that the questioner is the question itself, there is no question and no questioner. Full stop.

Q: There is a logic that comes in that says that if I don't think about it, then something might happen. It is that fear. I know you say the answers aren't in the mind, but if you think about something long enough, maybe you will arrive at a solution.

Bob: Well, have you?

Q: No. (Laughs)

Bob: How long are you going to think about something until that dawns on you that maybe the answer is not there?

Q: Yes. But it will be a thought that propels me to move eventually, when I do decide I'm going to go and do something.

Bob: Yes. But thinking comes up, with a so-called thought, from intelligence, and the movement happens from there. But the movement will happen without the thought also.

Q: Yes. I have seen that.

Bob: All the thought does is translate what is coming from that intelligence, puts it into words. The thought is just the labelling or translating what is happening in that pure intelligence. As I have said before, that so-called thinker or seer or hearer cannot do a thing of itself. The thought 'I see' cannot see. The thought 'I hear' cannot hear. The thought 'I think' is not the thinking.

From *Presence-Awareness*
Chap 36. P.121; The Mind Translates

Jeff Foster graduated in astrophysics from Cambridge University. Soon after graduation, life events propelled him onto an intense two-year spiritual search, culminating in the realisation that there was never anything to find in the first place. He currently writes and talks on what some people have called "nonduality", but which he just refers to as "the utterly, utterly obvious".

Life Without A Centre: Awakening from the Dream of Separation

168 pages. Isbn: 0-9553999-0-4 £7.95 / $13.95

Website

www.geocities.com/thisispresence/

"The vastness annihilates me. It literally destroys me. Walking through these empty streets, the vastness is there, consuming everything, every thought, every sensation. And yet the vastness is not separate from everything that is arising: the glow of the streetlamps, the shadows of lovers walking arm-in-arm, the rumble of night buses, the sound of footsteps on the cold pavement. And once again the secret that is so utterly obvious reveals itself: I am nowhere to be found, and I am everywhere. I am nothing, and yet I am one with all things, because there are not really any separate "things" at all."

"There are no words to do justice to the sheer beauty of this book, and its power of awakening resonance. I have only written two Amazon reviews to date, but cannot allow myself to pass on the chance to say a few words about this one. Over the past six years I have read many wonderful books on Advaita and non-dualism, but have never encountered the unavoidable sense of ever-present aliveness reflected in such a clear, direct and uncontrived way as in Life Without A Centre. Mr. Foster displays a unique style of writing which seems to effortlessly draw the apparent reader into a confrontation with his/her absence, that which is beyond the ability of the mind to grasp. This is a lively, spontaneous, lyrical, and often humorous, celebration in words of the simplicity of presence beyond the need of understanding. If you have read all the rest on this subject, then you deserve to read *Life Without A Centre*. Thank you, Jeff, for this gift that I know you will say "just wrote itself."

Amazon Reviewer

"In this short, brilliant book, Jeff Foster clearly shows that spiritual seeking is futile and pointless, since what we are seeking – awakening, liberation, the Ultimate Reality, etc. – is fully present now, yet we fail to see this because our minds are always searching for some better, happier state. By noticing that the mind is always searching for something better, we may find that the search relaxes, and that 'Liberation is just this, now.' Or to put it more bluntly, 'Liberation is staring you in the face.'

Jeff Foster expresses this message in such a clear, direct, light-hearted way that it seems obvious and impossible to ignore or refute. Many books about non-dualism and awakening leave one with the feeling that 'I haven't got it yet' and so encourage one to continue searching, but this book does the opposite. I strongly recommend it to anyone who does not want to continue seeking for the rest of their life."

Amazon Reviewer

I am alone in the garden. The sun is rising. A little robin tugs at a worm in the grass.

In true love, there is no object of desire, affection and tenderness; for the object of desire, affection and tenderness, the beloved, has collapsed into the lover. The object has collapsed into the subject, and there is only love: only love, and nobody to be aware of it; nobody to know it and nobody to deny it. Only love, both radically alone, and intimately connected to all things...

For a subject and an object can never be in love; they are forever divided from each other, split from each other; they can only gaze longingly into each other's eye across an unbridgeable divide, with the fervent hope that one day, one day, love will bridge the chasm, and the isolation of multiplicity and fragmentation will give way to the joy of intimate companionship, togetherness, unity. But no, love cannot and will not bridge the gap, for the gap is inherent in the subject-object split; indeed, the gap *is* the subject-object split, and nothing can fill a gap which is so deeply and fundamentally engrained into the very foundations of our experience. No, love cannot bridge the gap, because a subject and object, a lover and the beloved, are inherently, fundamentally separate. It is unlikely they will ever truly meet as people, as human beings.

But true love is the death of this terrible divide, and with it, the ending of all division between two people. But this will never be achieved through effort. The very effort to end the division strengthens the division, gives power to the division. For the division is not there. It has never been there, and it will never be there. The division is an illusion, and when you fight an illusion you must always lose.

Lovers will never meet through effort, though they may die trying.

*

So, our lovers continue to gaze longingly at each other across this unbridgeable divide, a divide that they unwittingly have created for themselves. How to help them? Any effort they would make to come together will pull them more strongly apart. Are they doomed to live and die like this? Is there a way out?

There is, but it involves death. Not physical death, but death of the ego; death of everything that separates, death of everything that fragments, death of everything that divides, death of everything that isolates, death of everything that has been carried over from the past, death of everything that projects into the future. Death of the idea of love itself. And finally, finally, it will involve death of the beloved, death of the lover. Death of you and me, and with it, death of all that comes between us. A descent into pure nothingness, a plunge into the unknown.

A risk.

And he who risks in this way may taste it; the sweet and simple joy of radical aloneness that is true love. Look! The robin tweet-tweets as he hops over dew-stained grass, as the morning sun begins to warm and wake the slumbering creatures in this Garden of Eden we have named Earth, and nowhere can I find isolation, loneliness, separation; but all things are in all things, and everywhere is mother, everywhere is home.

And I smile to myself with the realisation of the utterly, utterly obvious: I have not found you, but I have recognised something that has eluded me for a lifetime: *You are not out there, but in here. You are part of the experiencing structure I take to be myself.* And so I do not love you, for there is no "me" to love and no "you" to be loved. No, I do not love you; for you are part of that which loves...

From *Life Without a Centre*
P.151; On Love and Aloneness

Works by Jean Klein

Jean Klein, master of Advaita Vedanta in the tradition of Ramana Maharshi and Atmananda Krishna Menon, spent several years in India going deeply into the subjects of Advaita and Yoga. In 1955 the truth of non-dualism became a living reality. From 1960 he taught in Europe and later in the United States.

Publication of *Be Who You Are* and *Who Am I?* will be followed by *Beyond Knowledge, I Am* and *Living Truth.* These much sought after books, by one of the most important exponents of Advaita in recent years, are now available again from Non-Duality Press.

Be Who You Are

Translated by Mary Mann

Be Who You Are is one of the earliest published books of dialogues with Jean Klein. Written in the lucid and eloquent style which characterises his work, each chapter is composed of an introductory discourse followed by questions and answers.

ISBN 978-0-9551762-5-8 p.108 $11.95 / £7.45

Who Am I?

Compiled and edited by Emma Edwards

Unique among Jean Klein's works, the dialogues contained in this book have been organised by subject. Topics include: Relationship; The Nature of Thinking; The Art of Listening; A conversation on Art, etc.

ISBN 978-0-9551762-6-5 p.200 $16.50/£ 8.95

Beyond Knowledge

Compiled and edited by Emma Edwards

"During these meetings, be open to the openness, allow yourself to be deeply impregnated by the sayings that come directly from life. To be impregnated, the mind must be free from wrong knowing, that is, free from imposing an independent existence on all that is objective. Nothing that can be known has existence in itself. It depends on a knower. The knower is consciousness. Only consciousness never changes. We must find out what never changes in us."

Beyond Knowledge is a crystallization in word-form of this timeless wisdom. To read these dialogues is to enter into a scale of inquiry and clarity that knows no compromise. It carries one through to the end of thought and to the beginning of self-knowledge.

ISBN 978-0-9551762-8-9 p.164 $16.45 / £8.60

I Am

Compiled and edited by Emma Edwards

What you are looking for is what you already are, not what you will become. What you already are is the answer and the source of the question. In this lies its power of transformation. It is a present actual fact. Looking to become something is completely conceptual, merely an idea. The seeker will discover that he is what he seeks and that what he seeks is the source of the inquiry."

ISBN 978-0-9551762-7-2 p.164 $16.45 / £8.60

Living Truth

Compiled and edited by Emma Edwards

In the late 1980s Jean Klein was invited to give seminars in the Santa Cruz Mountains of California. In this isolated, peaceful mountain setting, a small group of students gathered with their life questions. The conversations of the 1988 seminar were transcribed and printed as a pamphlet entitled Mount Madonna Dialogues, but it was felt that the contents of all of the seminars were rich and rewarding enough to be gathered into a more substantial publication. 'Living Truth' is the result.

ISBN: 978-0-9553999-1-6 p.266 $19.95 / £10.95

Forthcoming Projects

Listening

Between 1989 and 1995 the Jean Klein Foundation published a series of ten Journals entitled *'Listening'*. These journals contained previously unpublished dialogues and prose pieces by Jean Klein together with a chosen selection of his favorite writings from other sources.

We hope to publish a complete compilation of these journals in book form in the autumn of 2007.

New Authors & Titles for

Summer/Autumn

2007

Jan Kersschot graduated in medicine from Antwerp University, Belgium. His lifelong quest for the ultimate truth was characterised by his interest in a wisdom which does not exclude anything or anyone. Blending the core of Eastern wisdom with a contemporary Western lifestyle, Jan shows in this collection of extraordinary dialogues how the popular myths about self inquiry and enlightenment can be unmasked. He is the author of the books, *Coming Home, Nobody Home* and *This Is It.*

The Myth of Self-Enquiry

120 pages. Isbn: 978-0-9553999-6-1 Price: £7.95 / $13.95 p/b

Website

www.kersschot.com

Publication date: July 7th 2007

"Probably you believe you are a person reading these very words right now. Maybe you also see yourself as a spiritual seeker. You've been to sacred places, followed yoga or meditation, maybe you've been involved in a group of seekers with similar interests. Probably you've invested a lot in this search for the ultimate truth. Maybe you feel you have been close to finding your true nature, and still ... something is lacking.

What if this search leads you nowhere because the seeker who wants to achieve "it" is itself a concept? Have you ever investigated the existence of the investigator you believe you are?

The seeker you believe yourself to be will not like this book. Seekers do not want to learn that that their search for enlightenment is just a game of their ego. They don't like to see that their spiritual enquiry is endless and that their goal of finding their "true nature" is a myth."

John Astin lives in northern California with his wife and daughter. Along with his work as a scientist studying the role of meditative practices in medicine and health care, he is a songwriter and recording artist, and the author of *Too Intimate for Words*. This second collection of poetic reflections on the nature of non-dual awareness is an exquisite collection of verses and prose writing.

This is Always Enough

140 pages. Isbn:978-0-9553999-5-4

Website

www.integrativearts.com

Publication date: August 3rd 2007

"Would you be willing to abandon, even for one instant, all teachers and teachings, all injunctions and practices, to simply meet what appears in each moment with no guidance or reference points to tell you what is true, or how you must live? What would it be like to cease to locate yourself in any teaching or teacher, to no longer be identified with any conceptual framework or spiritual philosophy – not yours, not Buddha's, not Jesus', not anyone's? How would it feel to live with no maps, no mental conclusions, no final destinations, to cease to refer to any notion in the mind about how anything is supposed to be?

We seek God but there is no escaping God for there is only God, only Spirit dancing as everything that is seen, everything that is touched, everything that is felt. We search for something else that will make us happy, some other experience or moment, but the happiness and freedom we seek is already here as this– this experience, this state of mind, this moment. Every breath, every sensation, the clarity, the confusion, the seeking, and the end of seeking, all of them God, all of them the Truth, all of them, enough."

From *This is Always Enough*

Jeff Foster's second book is a follow-up to his very well received first collection of writings, *Life Without a Centre* (p.49). Further reflections, refractions and dialogues on the *play of appearances.*

Jeff holds monthly meetings in London and other parts of the U.K by invitation.

Beyond Awakening: The end of the Spiritual Search

152 pages. Isbn: 978-0-9553999-7-8

Website

www.geocities.com/thisispresence

Publication date: September 7th 2007

"This book is about the utterly obvious. It's about the spiritual search, and the frustrations surrounding it. It's about the tendency of the mind to create and pursue goals. It's about those ultimate goals we set ourselves: enlightenment, awakening, liberation, permanent happiness, and how these goals can never really be reached, because – and here's the great discovery – the individual, the one who would reach any goals in the first place, has no more reality than a presently-arising belief. Which is to say, the individual does not really "exist" at all.

Yes, this is really a book about nothing, but still, sometimes a book about nothing can be the most helpful thing, when the search for something has only ever led to frustration and bitter disappointment.

But to read these words with a goal in mind – that would be to miss the point entirely."

Ordering Information

All book titles are available to order from most bookshops quoting the ISBN number, title and author. All titles are stocked by Watkins Books in Charing Cross Road, London and online from Amazon.co.uk and Amazon.com in the United States.

Wanuskewin in Amsterdam also stocks many of the Non-Duality Press titles.

Bookstores and Trade Customers
Trade enquiries to Non-Duality Press via their website: www.non-dualitybooks.com or to Bertram Book Group, Gardners and Bookspeed in the UK and Ingrams and New Leaf in the U.S.

LaVergne, TN USA
30 July 2010
191525LV00001BA/117/A

9 780955 399930

Books in Print

What's Wrong with Right Now?, Sailor Bob Adamson

Presence-Awareness, Sailor Bob Adamson

Awakening to the Dream, Leo Hartong

From Self to Self, Leo Hartong

Already Awake, Nathan Gill

Being: the bottom line, Nathan Gill

Awakening to the Natural State, John Wheeler

Shining in Plain View, John Wheeler

Right Here, Right Now, John Wheeler

You were Never Born, John Wheeler

This is Unimaginable & Unavoidable, Guy Smith

Perfect Brilliant Stillness, David Carse

Oneness, John Greven

I Hope You Die Soon, Richard Sylvester

Awake in the Heartland, Joan Tollifson

Be Who You Are, Jean Klein

Who Am I?, Jean Klein

I Am, Jean Klein

Beyond Knowledge, Jean Klein

Living Truth, Jean Klein

You were Never Born, John Wheeler

Life Without a Centre, Jeff Foster